HELLO
MY NAME IS

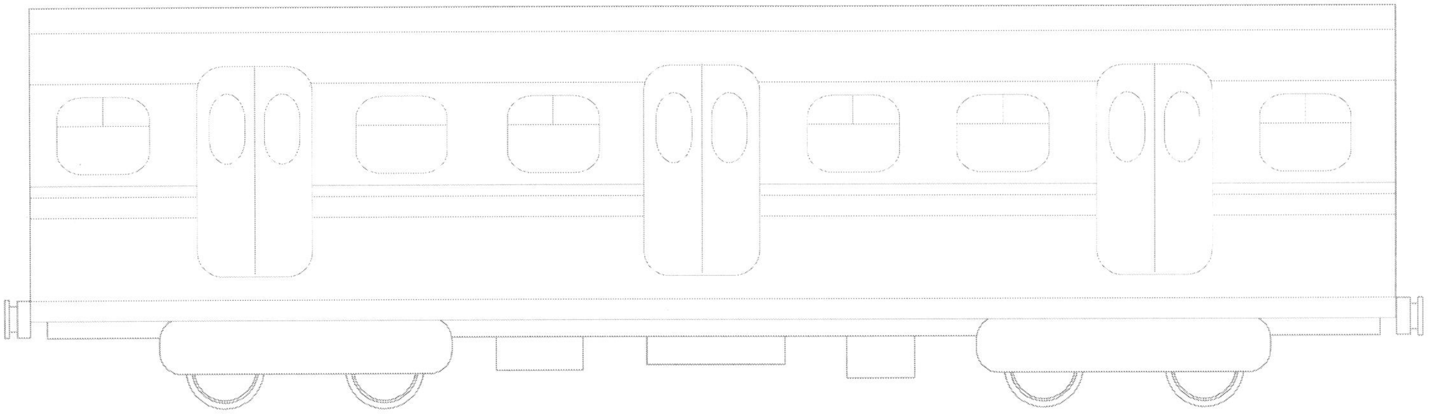

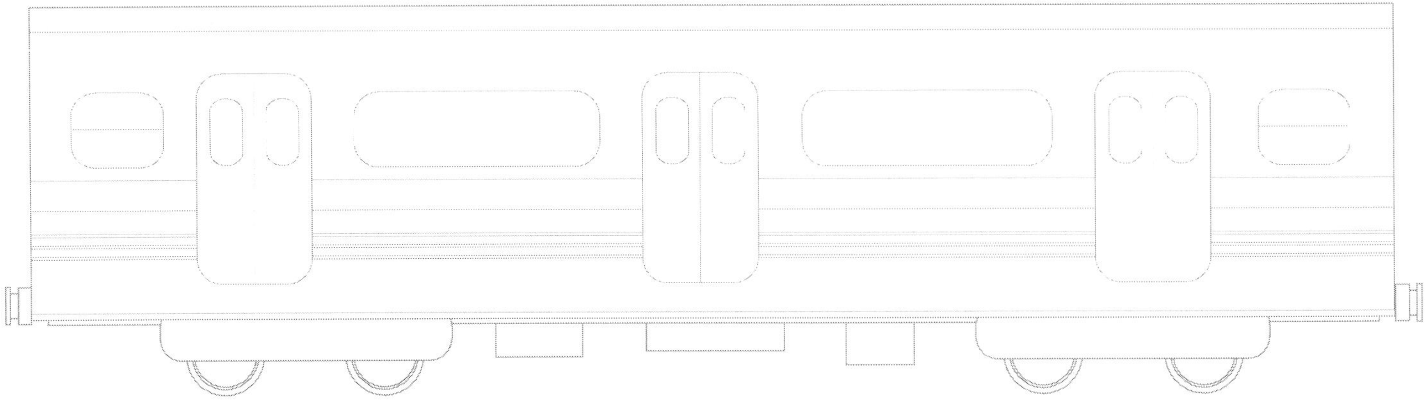

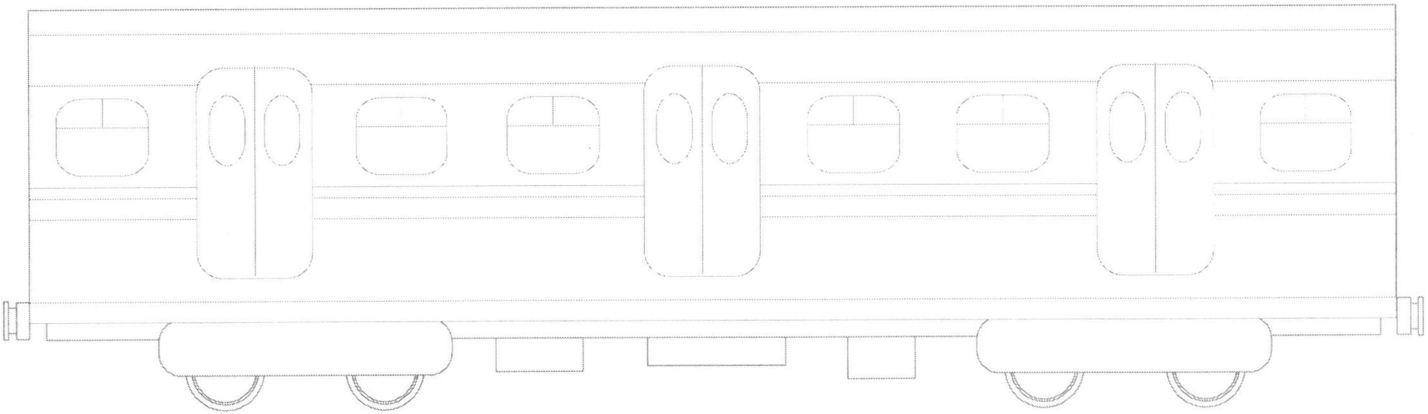

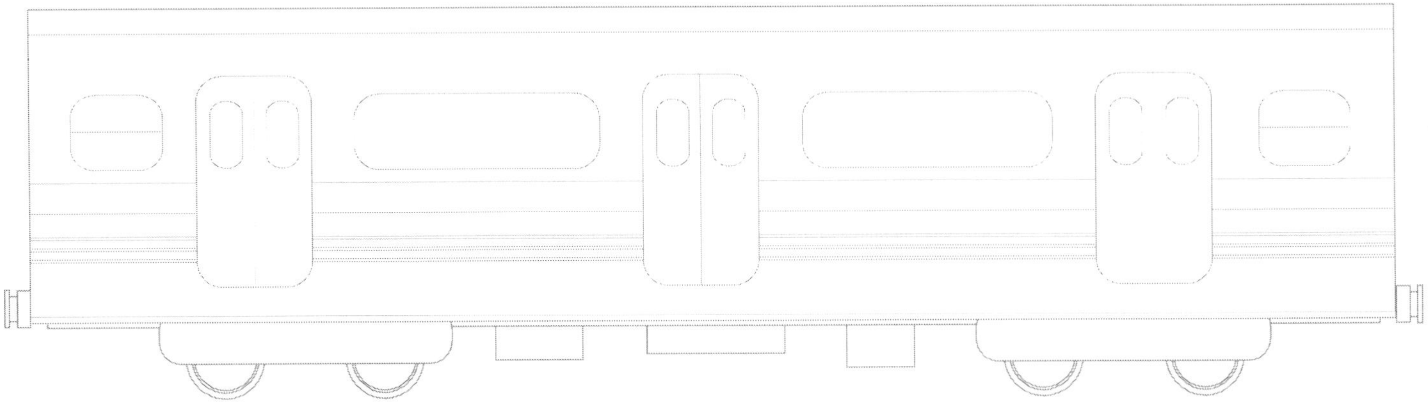

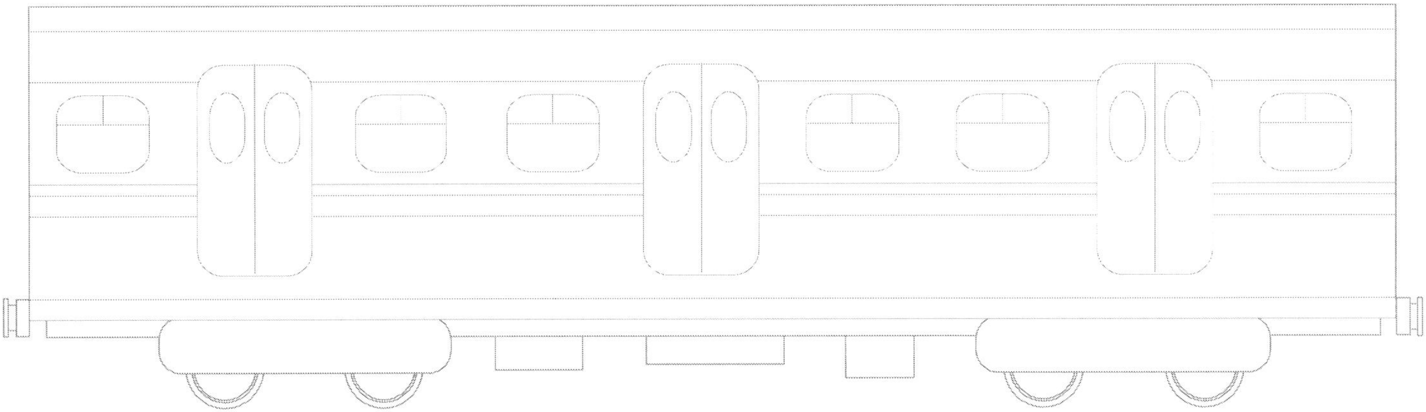

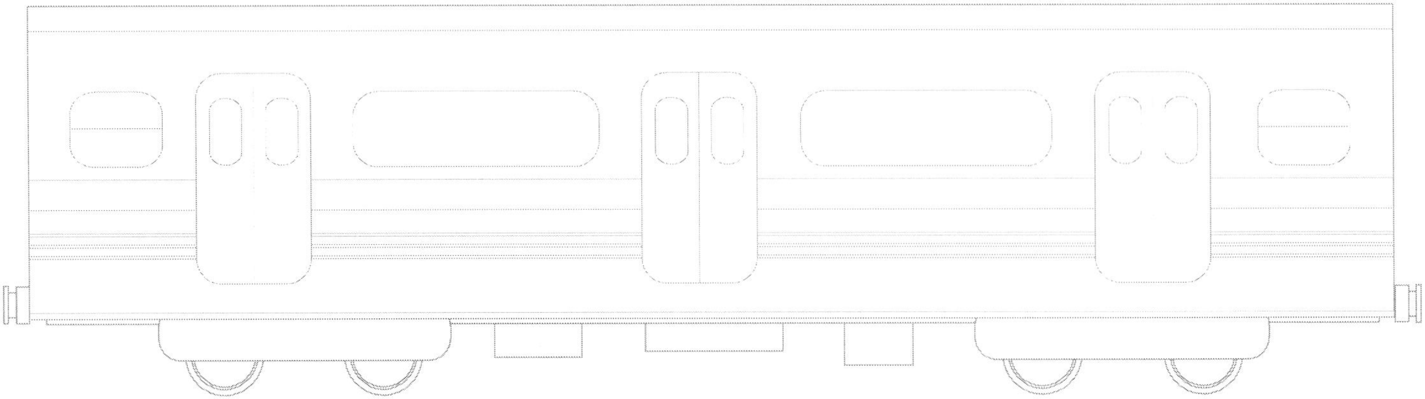

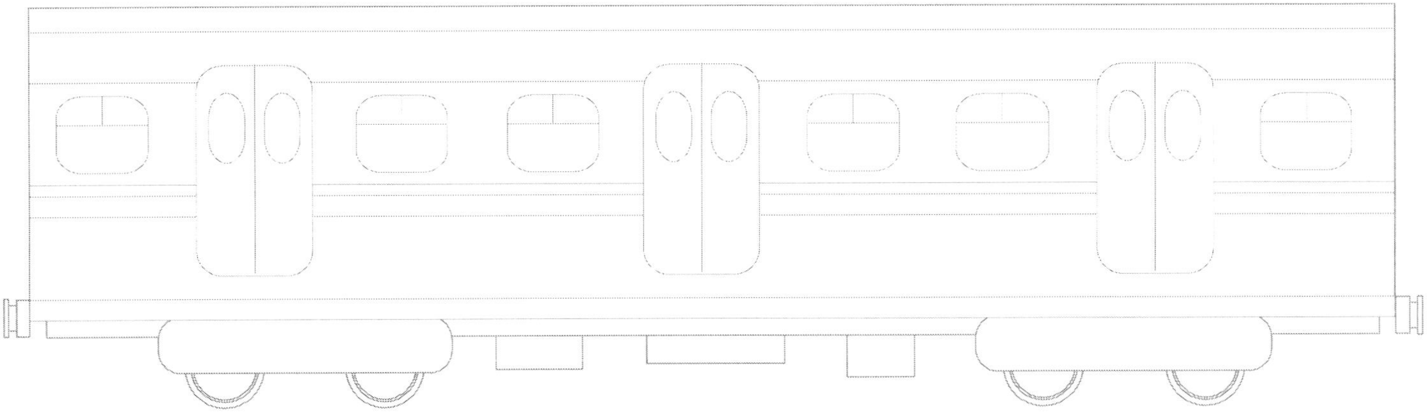
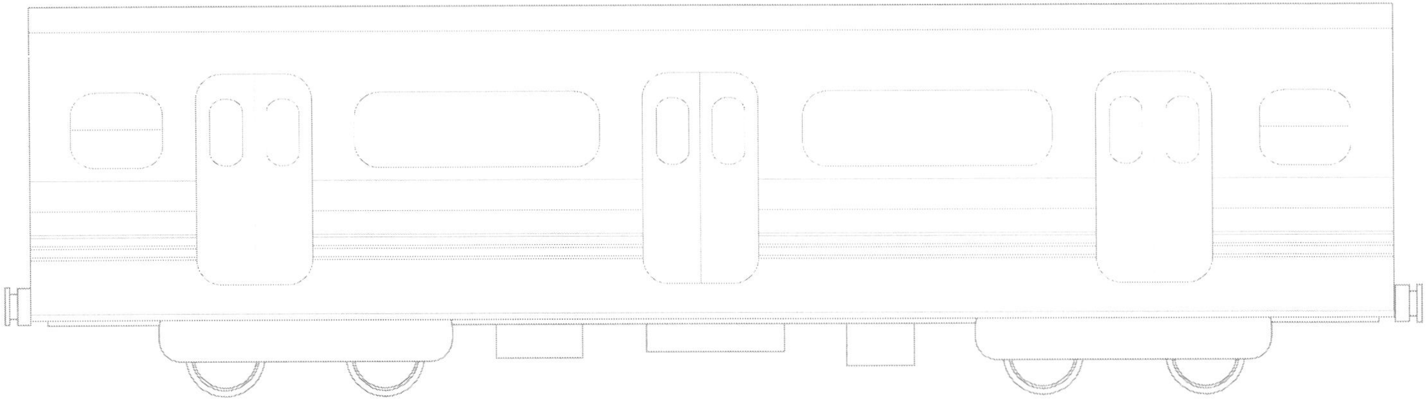

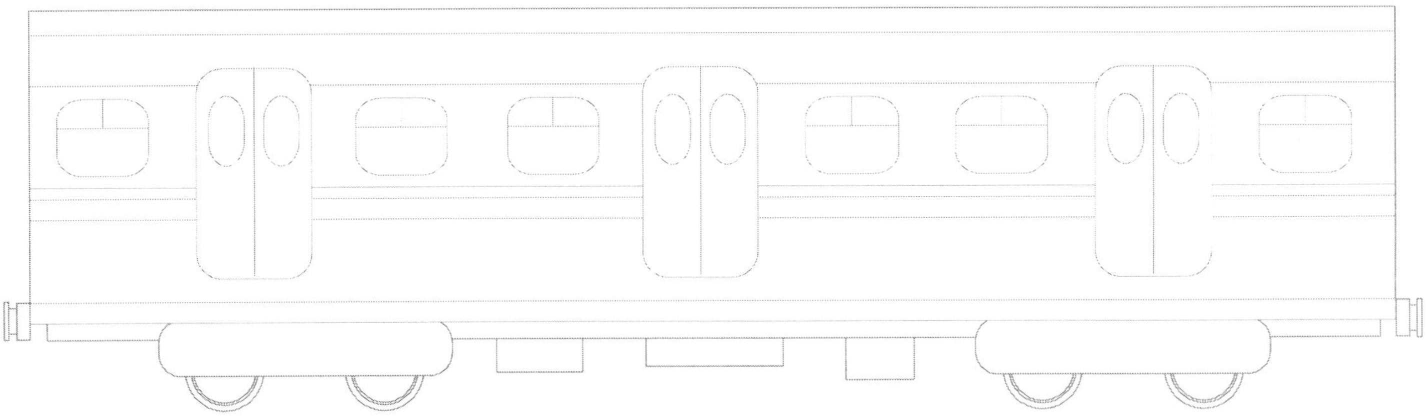

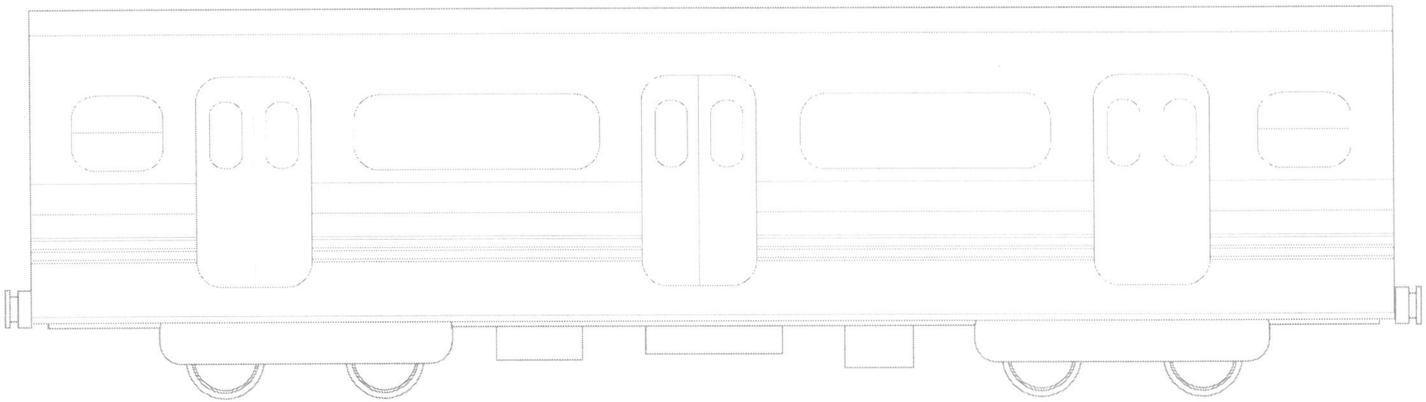

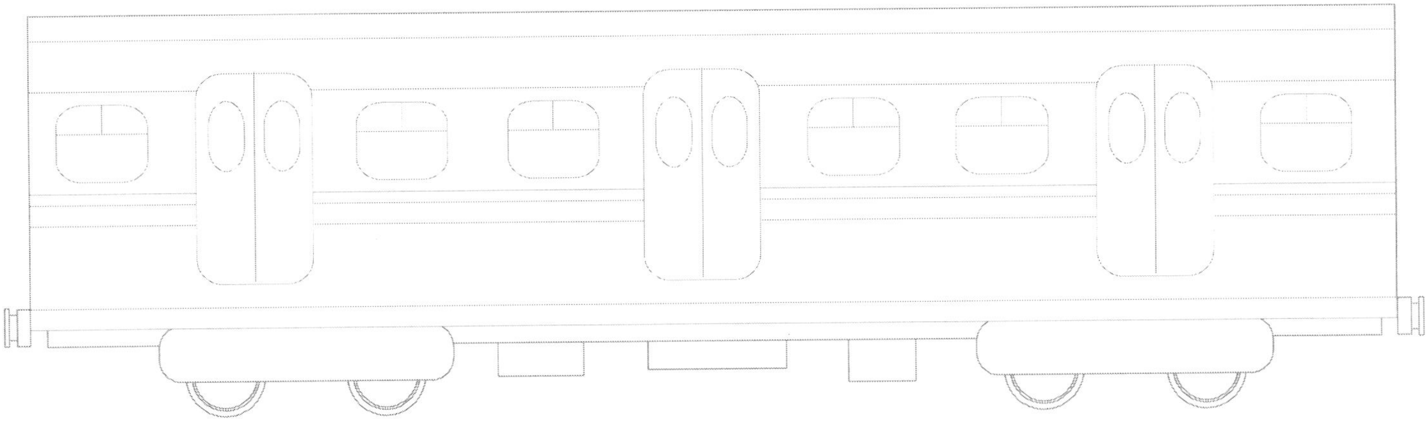

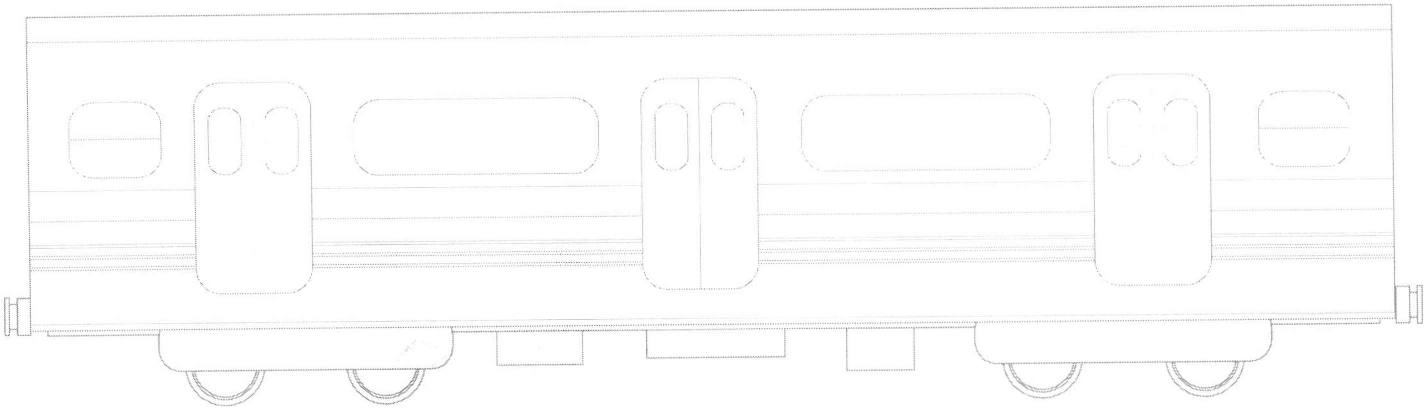

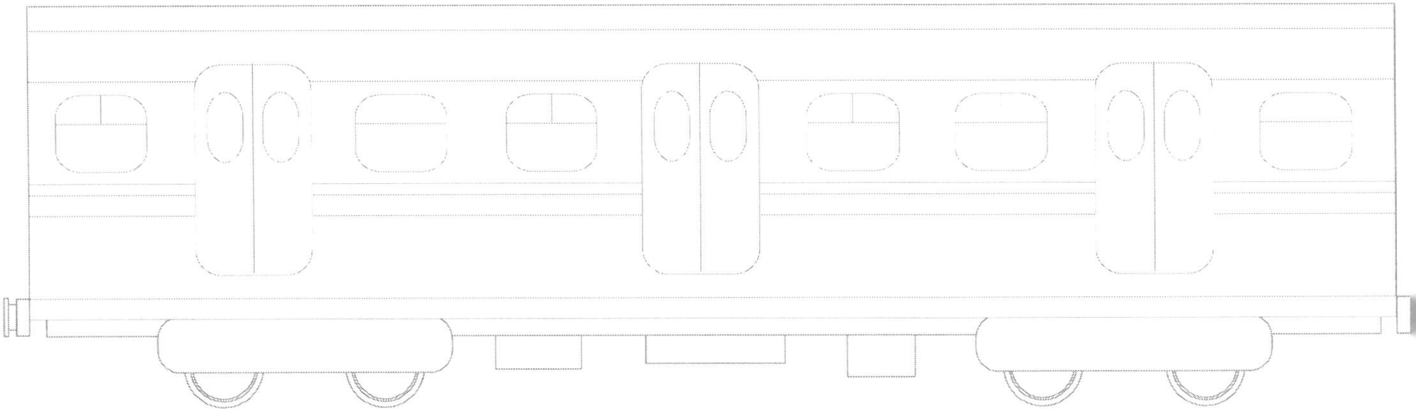

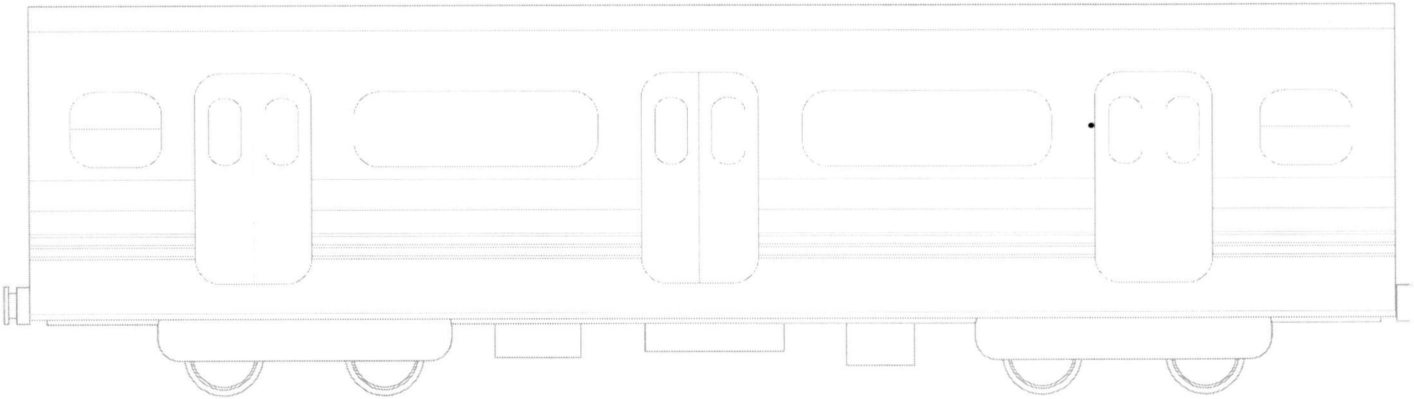

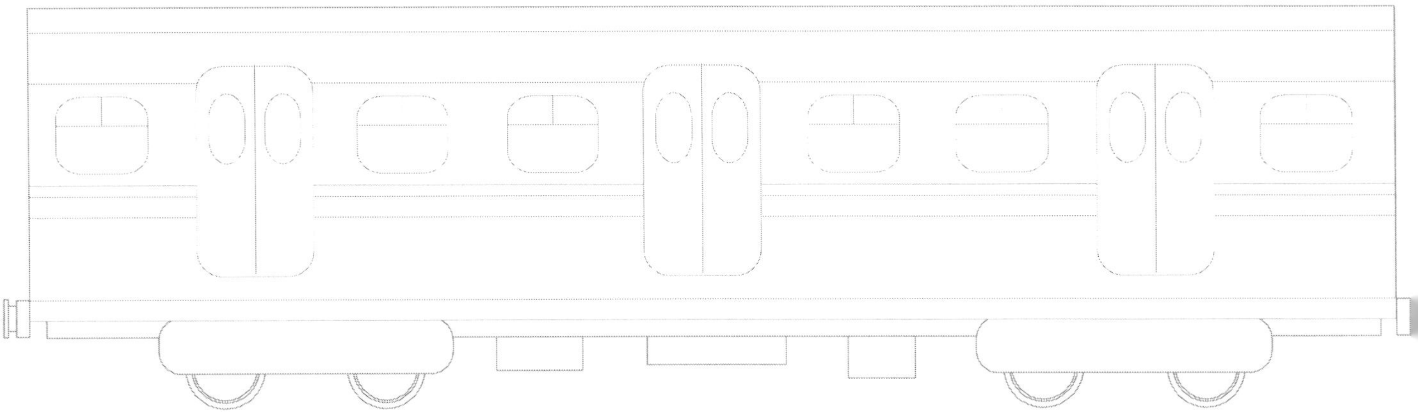

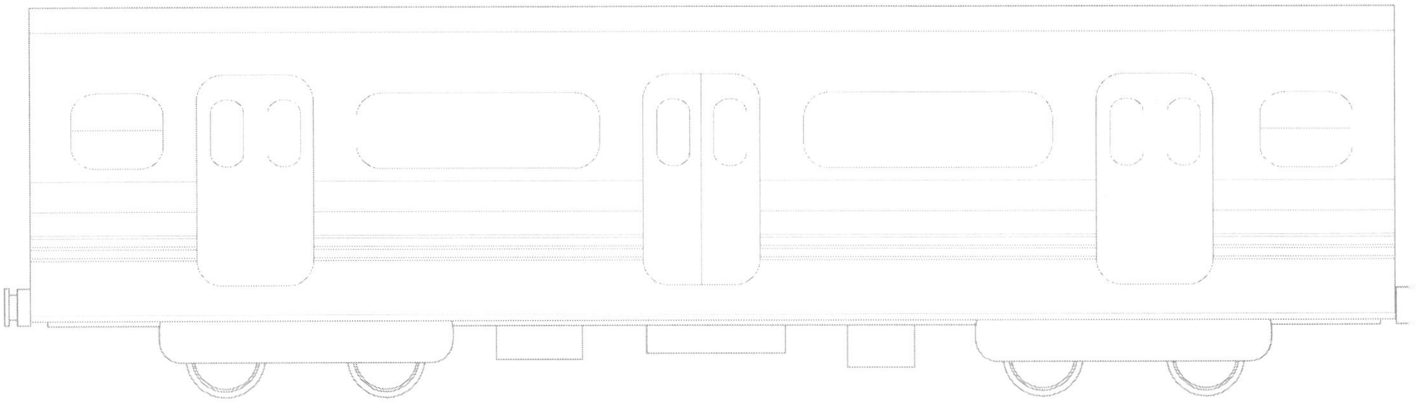

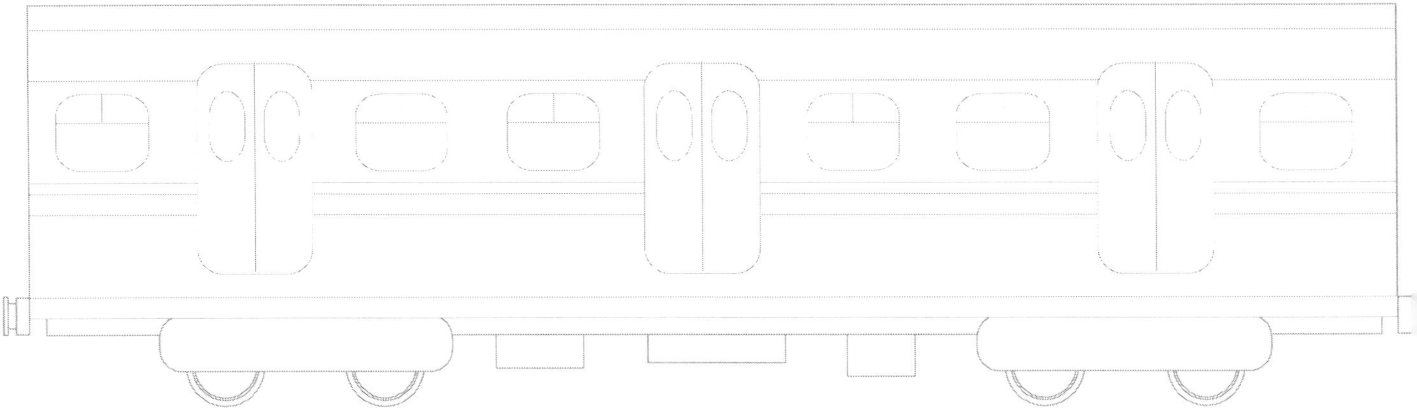

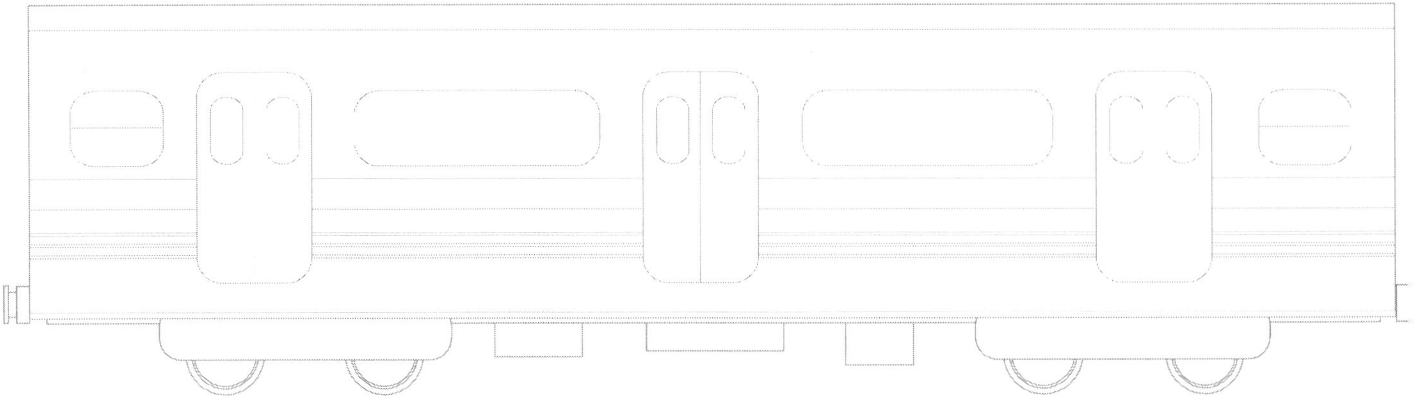

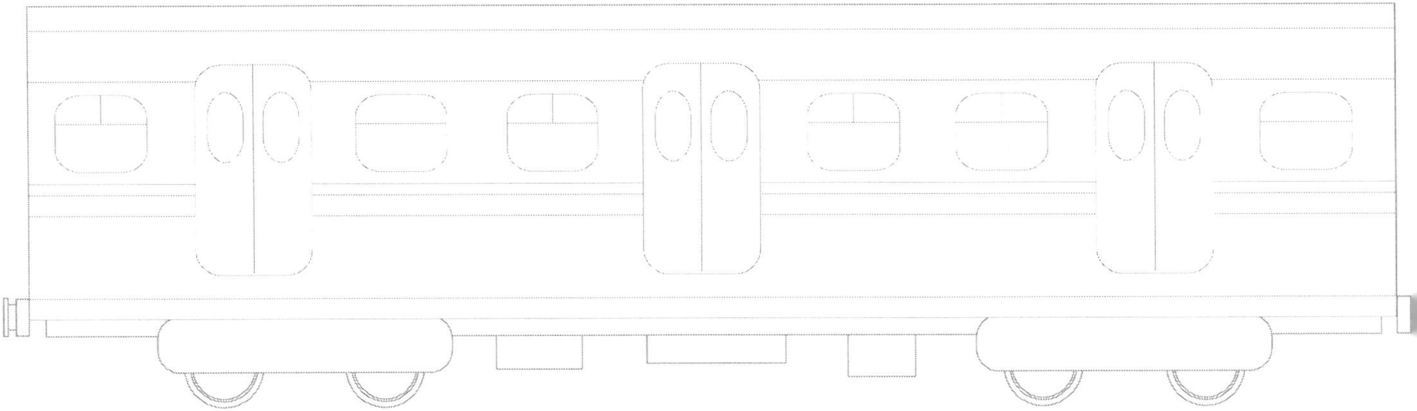

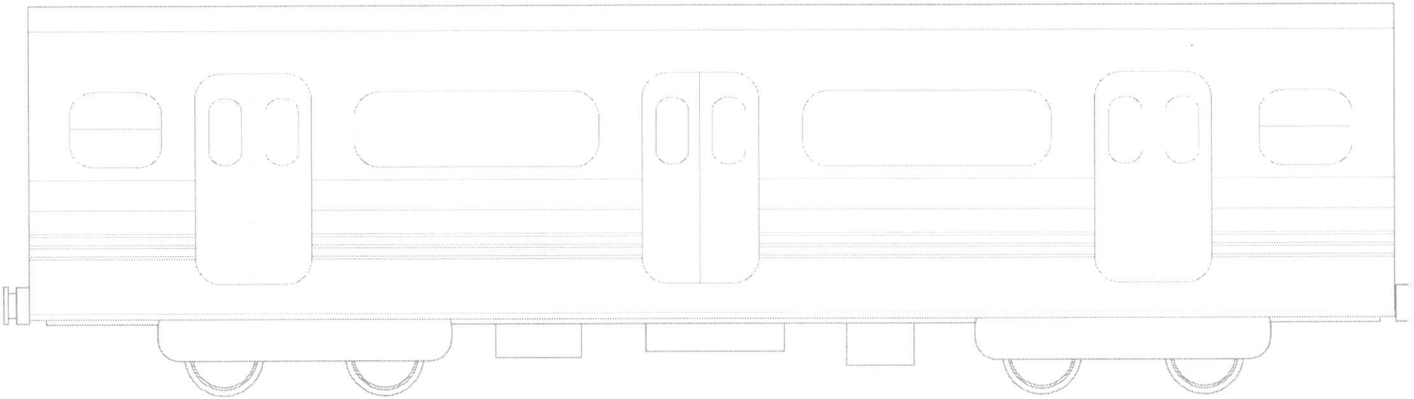

Printed in Great Britain
by Amazon

24451636R00058